The Performance Manifesto

" 7 Steps to Brilliant Performance"

By Daragh Sheridan

Published by: Sheriff Publishing, 2014
ISBN:978-0-9930933-0-2

Visit http://www.theperformancemanifesto.com/ to find out more about the author

To Susan, Dylan and Jack thanks for all the fun.

Contents

Introduction

I would like to welcome you to The Performance Manifesto. The aim of this book is to help you improve your performance in the everyday tasks, as well as more challenging opportunities of your life. In work it will help you in situations such as presentations, meetings, interviews & sales pitches etc. In your private life it will help you in your relationships, hobbies, sports, family, fitness etc. This is done by teaching you simple techniques that are easy to employ every single day of your life. You will learn sports psychology, Neuro Linguistic Programming (NLP) and hypnotic techniques that are normally used by sports people to improve their performance.

I, like most people, want to perform well and be good at whatever I do. Hell, I want to be more than good. I want to excel. In my case I want to be successful in my business and my sport of sailing. I also want a happy and content personal life. I am a qualified hypnotherapist and NLP practitioner. I have read many books, completed various programmes about self improvement, sports psychology and performance and enjoyed them all. I always learnt something from each and every one of them which is fantastic. The problem I had is that I struggled to put all these great ideas into my performance on a consistent basis.

I forgot things. I made the same mistake over and over again. I didn't use the right technique I had learned or I applied it in the wrong manner. I plain just didn't bother. Why did I do this? The simple answer is that it is human nature to do all of the above. While reading and learning these ideas I moved from one book to the next and from one programme to the next without really internalising the skills. I didn't make them my own so that I could call on them when I needed them, when I needed to perform at my very best. Why?

Because it was too much information.

I then discovered that many of my clients in my clinic had similar problems not only with their sporting performances but with more everyday tasks and challenges.

So I decided to devise a simple plan that fitted on a business card which I called "My Mentor Me Card" (MMM). This along with a simple technique and regular practice has enabled me to significantly improve my performance in all areas of my life. It has been fantastic. I have also used it with clients to help them improve in a wide range of different areas. I believe that this card will also improve your performance by changing your mental approach before, during and after any act, deed, or area that you are about to take part in. See Appendix 2 for an example of a MMM card for a presentation. Other examples of some of the MMM cards that my clients have used can be seen at www.theperformancemanifesto.com .

This My Mentor Me Card is the solution to excellent performance in all areas of your life. I have written a short User Guide to accompany the "Card" which explains how to use it and a simple description of each point. It is a no nonsense approach. This is in Appendix 1 which will allow you to use the system immediately. For those who like more detail, read the book – it's less than 80 pages long.

I would like to take this opportunity to thank those who taught me about the mind and how best to utilise it. Some taught me in person while with others it was via their books, audios, videos or online, and some taught purely by example. In no particular order thanks to Bob Proctor, Bob Rotella, Joe Keaney, Tony Robins, Gerry Robert, Vic Johnson, Dr Robert Anthony, Jim Fannin, Jason Selk, Dr Stephen Simpson, Brian Colbert, Ben Duncan, Anik Singal, Dr Steve Peters, Tony Horton and Shaun T.

I hope you enjoy it. I hope you use it to perform at the very top of your game be it sport, business, family or just life in general. I look forward to hearing about the results you achieve. Please feel free to check out www.theperformancemanifesto.com for further resources or to make contact with me.

The 1st Performance Step - "The Power Statement"

Self Talk

"Garbage in, Garbage out and Vice Versa"

Self talk is to the mind what food is to your body. If you put rubbish in you get rubbish out. I have put Self talk as the first step because it plays a vital part in all the other aspects of this programme.

Our self talk is critical in our belief about our ability to perform. It pervades what we do before, during and after performance. It's what we are saying to ourselves about ourselves, the situation, the competition, our team etc. Self talk to a large degree determines our level of confidence. Good, positive self talk leads to good, positive levels of confidence and vice versa which leads to excellent levels of performance. The cumulative effect leads to performing individual tasks better which will lead to a more successful life.

While I am advocating positive self talk and an optimistic outlook it is important that one is realistic about what they are trying to achieve, your talent and ability. No amount of positive self talk is going to make you win the Wimbledon Singles Tennis title when you are currently playing at the level of an average club player. On the plus side what is realistic may change over time as you acquire new skills and develop your ability in your area.

The problem most people experience is negative self talk. Negative self talk can manifest in the following ways:

- Thinking about negative outcomes.
- Not backing or believing your own ability.
- Inflating the competition's ability.
- Focusing on possible pitfalls or obstacles
- Not liking who we are.
- Fear of failure.
- Nervous talk.
- Living in the past.
- Lack of trust in ourselves.

The bottom line is that we can talk ourselves into anything good or bad. So we should concentrate on the good. However, this is easier said than done.

I have had the great honour of being Best man at the weddings of a few of my best friends. Most people would agree that public speaking is one of their greatest fears. Add in the expectation that a best man's speech should be funny and you have some serious pressure. I coped fine on the first couple of occasions and the speeches went off fine. You would assume that it would get easier each time I did it. This proved not to be the case. I was a nervous wreck the last time I did it. Why? What did I do differently?

The answer is that my self talk was less constructive than for the earlier occasions. I worried that I hadn't prepared well enough when in fact I had probably done more. I thought I didn't have the best material. I worried about the venue, the microphone and the audience. When I did the earlier speeches I concentrated on the positives like my friend and his big day with his gorgeous bride. I focussed on my delivery and what I could control.

Our self talk can tell us how we feel about ourselves, about our love of self. It is vitally important to love ourselves. It is a positive and good thing. I don't mean being conceited or self indulgent. I simply mean liking and enjoying who we are. It means accepting that we are not perfect and that we make mistakes. We have to remember how amazing we human beings are.

There are countless examples of people whose lack of self love resulted in tragedy. In most cases the lack of self love and positive self talk does not lead to such tragedy. It can however lead to poor performance. How can we improve our self talk and as a consequence improve our performance?

The Power Statement

I suggest that the best way to improve yourself talk and build your confidence is to produce your own unique *Power statement*. This is a short simple phrase, sentence or even just a number of keys words. The Power statement must contain the essence of what you believe you require to perform at your very best. You will need different statements for different areas that you are trying to improve. In order to illustrate this I will tell you the statement I use for sailing and then formulate some possible other examples to help you develop your own Power statement.

The key aspects for me to perform well in a sailboat race are that I keep my head out of the boat to see changes in conditions and situations that are coming down the racecourse at me, hopefully before my competition. Also it is vital for the performance of the boat that the boat is well balanced. A well balanced boat is a fast boat. Then the three elements I have found from experience that enable me to perform at my best is that I am calm, focussed and that I am having fun. So from this my Power statement is:

"Head out, calm, balanced, focussed & fun"

I use this in many different situations such as

- If I catch myself thinking negatively.
- Before competition.
- During a race if I have had an incident that has interrupted my concentration.
- During practice.
- During visualisation exercises.(more about this later)

In order to enhance the effectiveness of my Power statement I also use an anchoring technique. Anchoring uses a stimulus that may be a sound, an image, a touch, smell or a taste to trigger a consistent response in you or someone else. A good example of an anchor is when you hear a song from your past and it brings up a strong emotional feeling or memory. The way we are going to use anchors here is to deliberately link the anchor to the way we want to feel when we perform. I simply tap my thigh while repeating my power statement when I am feeling calm, balanced, focussed and having fun. With repetition I can then bring about these feelings at will by simply tapping my thigh. The combination of the anchor and the Power statement brings my desired state to me when I require it in the heat of competition. Any desired state can be created in the same manner for different situations.

In order to give you another example of the Power statement in action I decided to use the situation of giving a speech or a presentation. It is something a lot of people have problems with and come up against this challenge at some stage in their lives. I will use the presentation as the non sports performance example throughout this book but it could be any performance or task that you need help with.

The first decision you need to make is to choose your desired state. That is the way you want to feel while you make your speech. This includes the way you believe a speech should be for the given situation. A wedding speech will probably have a different desired outcome than a presentation to a group of your work colleagues. So for this example we will use the presentation to colleagues.

We want our presentation to inform, educate and be professional. We also want to be ready and prepared for discussion or questions at the end or during the presentation. Therefore some of the feelings or thoughts you might want to experience during it are to be professional, knowledgeable, clear, calm and aware. So your Power statement will contain those words or those words contained in a simple statement. So it could be "I am professional, knowledgeable, calm, clear and aware of my audience", or just the words "professional, knowledgeable, calm, clear and aware". A good anchor could be simply clasping your hands behind your back as you are experiencing these feelings.

So before moving on to the next chapter please prepare the following:

- Think of the state of mind you desire or the key attributes of a superb performance in whatever it is you are about to do.
- Think of words or a short phrase to use as your Power statement.
- Repeat your Power statement as often as you can. Do it during training, practice; during visualization exercises; during actual performances.
- Use an anchor to power up the effectiveness of your Power statement.
- Fill in Step 1 your Power Statement on you're my Mentor Me Card.

The 2nd Performance Step – "Visualisation on steroids"

Visualisation

"The secret of achievement is to hold a picture of a successful outcome in mind"

Henry David Thoreau

Visualisation is simply making pictures or movies in your mind. We do it all the time. The skill in performance terms is picturing yourself performing superbly. It is essentially practicing in your mind. This is based on the phenomena that when a person imagines doing something the neurons fire in the same way as they would when they are actually performing. As a result practicing in your imagination is almost as effective as real life practice. This has been borne out in studies.

Some of you may be aware of a study that was carried out at the University of Chicago. A number of students were divided into three groups. On the first day all students were tested shooting a number of foul shots in basketball. The groups then were given the following instructions:

- Group One was told not to play or practise any basketball for a month.

- Group Two were told was told to practice shooting baskets for an hour each day, every day, for the month.
- Group Three were told to spend one hour a day imagining they were successfully shooting baskets. Do this every day for the month. Imagine in their minds successfully shooting baskets. See every detail of your accomplishments in your mind.

After these 30 days a new test was done and compared with the results from day 1 as a reference, the new results were very surprising:

- Group 1 had 0% improvement, which is not very surprising.
- Group 2 improved 24%, which is not bad, but they had been training with the ball for 30 days
- Group 3 improved 23%, which is very surprising, since they had not touched the ball for 30 days.

Group 3, who had not set foot on a basketball court, who had only imagined shooting baskets in their mind, had improved their performance by a phenomenal 23%, almost the same improvement as the group who had actually played basketball!

These results depict the power of visualization and mental rehearsal.

Mental practice also improves our confidence by simply imagining ourselves performing successfully.

We create images in our heads all the time. So, how do we carry out this process in a way that helps us perform to the high standards we want?

Visualising "on Steroids"

In order to get the best out of your mental rehearsal or "visualise on steroids" you need do the following.

1. Visualise from your point of view

Always visualise your future performance through your own eyes. Some people find it easier to imagine that they have a camera on their head and this provides the pictures. It may be useful at times to visualise your performance from a third party view like looking down on your performance from overhead. This would be mainly in situations where you are trying to achieve an element of detachment from your actions. Most of the time however, it is best to see it through your own eye view. You may have seen this referred as "being associated".

2. Utilise all your senses

Visualisation works best when you can bring all your senses into the equation. The more senses you can use in your visualisation the more it imitates the actual situation. Experience it in as much detail as you can. I will use the example of a golfer. A golfer will visualise his shot from his point of view. He should also do the following

- Imagine the touch and feel of the club in his hands.
- Imagine feeling the temperature in the air if he is going to be playing in a warm climate.
- Imagine the smell of the fresh cut grass.
- Imagine hearing the sounds of the spectators.
- Imagine how he is feeling internally as he stands over his shot.

There may be situations where you can even imagine the taste and flavours of things, if you were a chef competing in a competition such as Masterchef.

3. Run the scenario all the way through.

You should always run your visualisation exercise all the way through from beginning to end. See yourself preparing at home at the start of the day through the actual performance and then see yourself at the end of the day going back through your performance.

4. Do it regularly.

This has proven to work best in short regular sessions. Ideally keep it under ten minutes but do it regularly.

5. Practice and do it until its right.

Sometimes you may find that something keeps going wrong in your visualisation exercises. Keep replaying it until you get it right.

6. Overcoming difficulties.

See yourself performing successfully. It is also important that you foresee challenges that may arise and visualise yourself dealing with them with aplomb.

7. Use past success.

Review past success during your visualisation exercise. Once again, get as many of your senses involved in remembering in detail your successful performances from the past.

How do we put a really effective visualisation session together? The following will form the basis of any session which you can customise to your own needs.

- Find yourself a nice comfortable chair or bed, close your eyes and allow yourself to relax completely. This can be something as simple as taking ten deep breaths or you can use a hypnotic induction. As I am a qualified Hypnotherapist I like to use hypnosis as I find it really enhances the quality and effectiveness of visualisation. I have included a brief hypnotic induction as an appendix to this book if you would like to try using it. It's a tremendously relaxing experience regardless of the outcomes you are looking to achieve. You can either record yourself reading the script in Appendix 3 or you can download a copy of my "Essence of Relaxation" recording at www.theperformancemanifesto.com

- Once you are relaxed begin visualising, remembering to use as many senses as you can. This can simply be imagining pictures in your mind or it may take the form of short movies. Some people find it helpful to imagine a television or cinema screen on which they can view the movies or pictures. I find it most useful to create short movies.
- First picture a number of high points from previous performances. This may be the race you got your best result in or it could be a time when you overcame significant obstacles. Pick two or three incidents and play the movie of them in your mind. When you get to the point in the movie where you feel really good, confident and powerful

repeat your Power statement and use your anchor.

- Pick your greatest ever achievement in your chosen field and imagine a movie of that.
- Then I want you to then project yourself into a movie of an upcoming performance or event. Imagine yourself performing at your very best, performing the way you want to. As with the past experiences use as many senses as you can. See yourself overcoming possible difficulties and implementing your contingency plans. Again use your Power statement and your anchor to initiate the feelings you want to have during performance.
- Then see yourself having achieved the success you are striving for. See the awards ceremony, hear the crowds cheering, see you and your team congratulating each other or see the audience applauding you on completion of your speech. Really enjoy this moment. Congratulate yourself.
- If you are doing something for the first time you obviously won't have the past experiences to draw on. In this case it is even more important to do the future movie

visualisation the way you want things to go in an ideal performance.

Finally it is really important to have fun with this. Your imagination and mind is an amazing thing and can create any picture or movie you want so go have fun with it. See your body and mind and spirit all performing to their optimum. It's daydreaming for adults!

Another cool thing to strengthen the impact of your visualisation is to practice while you sleep. Jim Fannin, the world renowned coach, uses this as an essential part of coaching to top sports people. This is a really powerful sports tool but works equally well in other areas.

Whatever you think about in the last 30 minutes before you go asleep is critically important. Whatever feelings, thoughts, sensations emotions you have are recorded and replayed 15-17 times during the night. Just imagine how fantastic or destructive this can be in your life. This explains why we have a bad night's sleep after an argument with a loved one just before bed. It explains the old saying of "never go to bed angry". Those angry or argumentative thoughts are replayed all night. On the flip side imagine going to bed thinking about positive things and feelings.

Imagine creating positive pictures in your mind about what you wish for and have those replayed. I guarantee you will wake up feeling better in the morning.

You don't need to do this for the entire 30 minutes before you go to bed. It only takes a couple of minutes. Just get yourself into a nice relaxed hypnotic state by doing some deep breathing then imagine the good things you want as already having happened. Simple!

So before moving on to the next chapter please prepare the following for an upcoming performance that you have.

- Select a few past successes that you are going to utilize in your visualization exercises.
- Think about feelings you want to experience during a superb performance in whatever it is you are about to do.
- Think of other senses you can use in your visualization. What will you see, hear, smell, touch and even taste if that is relevant.
- Decide on a time of day that you are going to do this, as it will benefit if you do it in short but regular sessions. Once a day for ten minutes or so should be fine.
- Fill in Step 2 on you're my Mentor Me Card.

The 3rd Performance Step - "Shake your Booty"

"Fear is excitement without the breath"

Fritz Perls

Body Language & Breathing

The state of mind we are in determines our behaviour and also our performance. We can change the way we feel by changing our physiology. Don't believe me? Try feeling down when you are smiling. Also try feeling happy when you have your head bowed toward the ground versus holding your head up high. Hell, it even became a phrase and lyric in a song to "hold your head up high" as a metaphor for rising to your challenges. Try feeling stressed when you perform deep breathing. We can change our state by changing our body in some way. This changes our feelings, which leads to a change in our performance. What can we do with our bodies to help improve our performance?

One of the great rivalries in tennis was that of the two legends John McEnroe and Bjorn Borg. The two men had some epic battles during the late 70's and early 80s in their quest to be the best men's tennis player in the world. While they were both amazing players they couldn't have been more different in the way they went about it. They illustrate perfectly how different people can use their physiology in completely different ways in order to achieve the performance level they want.

On one hand Borg remained icily calm using deep breaths and a cool stare to remain calm in the tightest of points during matches. He appeared to just amble around the court without a worry in the world. This calmness enabled him to never appear ruffled to his opponents and allowed him to move and perform to his very best. He went on to win six French opens in a row and five Wimbledon championships in a row along with one US Open.

McEnroe was the complete opposite; in order for him to perform at his best he needed to be fired up and boy did he get fired up. He was a real terrier on the courts pacing quickly and doing almost everything in an aggressive manner. He bashed his racquet on the ground, fired tennis balls away. This use of his body coupled with aggressive questioning of the umpire's calls enabled him to psych himself up to perform well. Everybody at the time would remember his "you cannot be serious" outburst. He went on to win three Wimbledon titles and four US Opens.

The two players had vastly different ways of using their bodies and speech or lack of speech to achieve their goals. Both were hugely successful. So it's simply a case of finding whatever works best for you as an individual.

Breathing

Most people tend to breath in quick sharp inhales and exhales. This is also the type of breathing that we do when we are stressed or under pressure. So the first thing we can do with our breathing is to use it to help us relax. We do this by using deep breathing or diaphragmatic breathing. It is simply breathing deep down into your stomach not just your chest. It reduces stress, increases the oxygen to your muscles and has a calming effect. There are a many ways to breathe deeply. Experiment and find out what works for you. The best way I have found is to

- inhale through your nose for five count
- hold for two count
- exhale for seven count

It can help if you place your hand on your stomach to feel it move in and out until you become practiced at it.

This breathing technique can be used:

- Just prior to performance or during performance.
- During visualisation exercises.
- It is also very useful as part of a "reset" to prepare for a second race or a break in performance like between games in a tennis match or between holes on a golf course. I will talk about this "reset" in more detail later in the book.

Move your Body

Simply move your body in a new way to create a different state of mind. Jump up out of your seat, run up and down the stairs and see how different you feel. It makes an immediate change to how we are feeling. I am not going to get into the science of it here but simply moving releases chemicals into the body that create a natural high and having us feeling great and ready to perform at our best.

You can develop movements that will help you in your own particular performances. Examples are a tennis player doing a few quick jumps up and down to create a peak performance state. Another one could be somebody about to give a speech rubbing their hands together or clapping to create that altered frame of mind.

Ideally these movements should be used alongside the Power statement and our anchors that I have mentioned earlier.

Exercise and Nutrition

This book is about performing superbly in all areas of your life. It is suffice to say that being fit and eating well enhances our performance regardless of the arena we are performing in.

Before you move on to the next chapter please do the following:

- Practice deep breathing.
- Decide on a couple of deliberate movements you will use during performance to create the state you want.
- Exercise and eat healthily.
- Write in the actions you will use in Step 3 of your My Mentor Me Card.

The 4th Performance Step - "Be Here Now"

Focus

"Concentrate all your thoughts on the work at hand. The sun's rays do not burn until brought to a focus"

Alexander Graham Bell.

Focus on the now we have always been told. It is easier said than done. People that perform at the very top level in their fields manage to do this one thing more often than not. The average performer struggles to stay in the now. Their minds and their focus flits from one thought to the next. They often think about the outcome, external factors or other things they have no control over.

There is a famous story about the legendary golfer Arnold Palmer in the 1961 Masters tournament. Palmer lead the field by one shot and had just hit a good drive up the last. He was approached by a friend who shook his hand and said "you won it". This small gesture resulted in Palmer losing his focus and took his mind out of being in the moment. It resulted in him making a six and handing the win to Gary Player. So if one of the greatest golfers of all time struggled to stay focussed and in the moment, how are mere mortals expected to do it?

There are a number of things we can do to help us stay focussed.

1. Keep calm

By keeping calm we increase our ability to focus on what needs to be done at a given time. We can do this by simply focusing internally on our breathing or on relaxing a part of our body. As mentioned elsewhere you can download my audio "The Essence of Relaxation" at www.theperformancemanifesto.com

2. Focus on a process not an outcome.

By focusing on a particular process involved in your performance you will avoid thinking about the outcome. Thinking about the outcome is what led to Arnold Palmer's loss in the story above.

So a golfer should concentrate on his current shot and the processes involved until there are no more holes left to play. Ideally he would not take into account his score or position in the tournament until he adds it up after his last shot.

A great example of a process goal was British Open champion, Louis Oosthuizen's small red dot on his glove. He credited this small red dot with playing a critical role when he won the Open. The intention was to help the South African to concentrate on his swing in the crucial moments leading up to a shot. It allowed Oosthuizen, a rank outsider, to handle the intense pressure of the final round of a major championship and to focus on his swing.

The idea came from Karl Morris a sports psychologist who was asked to help Oosthuizen with his concentration after he had a string of disappointing results. The plan was to focus on the red dot during his swing. This enabled him to focus on the task in hand, the hitting of the golf shot rather than any of the myriad of things that could be going through the head of a potential major champion. It critically allowed him to remain in the here and now.

Similarly somebody giving an important speech could focus on the cadence of his voice and on his breathing and not on the impact that his speech might or might not have on his audience.

3. Focus on what you can control.

It is critical for you to focus on things that are within your control. This is essential in sports like my sport of sailing. There are so many variables that I have no control over: the wind, the sea, the tides and what my competitors do. All I can do is to focus on controlling my reaction to each of these variables. This applies to all areas of performance where there are the variables of nature. It is also essential where there are other competitors, rivals or even team mates whose actions you cannot control.

4. Don't evaluate or judge

During performances it is really important that you are not judging or critiquing your performance as it happens. You must trust yourself to perform to the best of your ability at that moment. If you are judging you are not fully engaged in the process. Leave your evaluation of the performance until after where you can really learn something from it.

So before moving on to the next chapter please do the following for your own performance, sporting or otherwise.

- **Use a combination of breathing and your Power statement to concentrate on a particular action of your performance. For example a golfer might take a deep breath and then say "smooth and natural" as he exhales and takes his swing.**
- **Come up with something like the red dot that Louis Oosthuizen used to focus on your process and to ignore distractions.**
- **Develop a ritual including your Power statement and anchor to the feeling of being intensely focussed while being relaxed.**
- **Prioritise what actions you need to focus on and try and keep them to a small number.**
- **Learn from past experience and performance.**
- **Try to foresee possible distractions and plan how you are going to deal with them.**

- **Complete Step 4 of your My Mentor Me Card with your chosen point of focus.**

**The 5th Performance Step- "Daydreaming for adults"
(Feel like a winner)**

Confidence and Belief

"Whether you think you can, or you think you can't, you're right"

Henry Ford

Achieving your best requires confidence in your ability to perform at a high level. Confidence is the feeling or belief that you can do something well. We all are confident at doing some things and not so confident in other areas. Confidence for some is bravado and being showy. For others it is a quiet determination and resolve. Why does it differ from person to person?

I believe it differs because confidence is the emotion we as an individual want to feel during our performance. So therefore it will differ from person to person and it will also differ depending on what we are doing. The feeling of confidence in an American football player would be quite different to that of a chess player or somebody about to sit an exam. So what is the feeling of confidence that we want to feel for most situations?

I believe the best way to describe feeling confident is a "winning feeling and a belief we can do what we set out to do". For most people and situations this is generally a feeling of joy at your success. However, confidence could refer to other feelings depending on what we wish to achieve. Another example would be a feeling of calm and relaxation resulting from a performance. It all depends on what we as an individual want to feel and what we believe we need to feel to be successful. For the purposes of the book I will continue to describe it as a winning feeling.

The easiest way we can create belief and confidence is by using our amazing minds and imaginations. We should recall times in the past when we felt confident. Remember those feelings and use our imagination to feel confident in the situation we face in the future. We don't necessarily have to have experienced it in our past. The feeling of confidence comes from within ourselves. We can use our imagination to create that winning feeling. The winning feeling plus our imagination leads to confidence and success.

When you feel confident and successful you will act so.

Another way of creating a winning, confident mentality is by using what Neuro Linguistic Programming (NLP) called sub modalities. This way of changing how we feel was brought to us by the founders of NLP Richard Bandler and John Grinder. Basically they refer to the five sensory systems as being modalities. These can be broken down further into what they referred to as sub modalities. Some examples of sub modalities are:

Visual

Brightness, size, color, shape, location, distance, contrast, focus, clarity, movement, speed, three-dimensional/flat, perspective, associated/disassociated, framed/panoramic, orientation.

Hearing

Pitch, cadence, volume, rhythm, timbre, clarity, location, distance.

Feeling

Pressure, location, frequency, texture, temperature, intensity, vibration etc.

So people will have different sub modalities for a given situation and will have different sub modalities for positive experiences and thinking to those they experience for negative experiences and thinking. So the key to changing your bad or negative feelings is to change the sub modalities associated to it.

In order to do this, think of something you like doing or feel good doing and note all the sub modalities connected to it. Now think of something you feel negatively about doing and note all the sub modalities attached to it. Some sub modalities for both will be the same, whereas some may be different. The trick now is to change or swap-over the sub modalities for a negative feeling to the same sub modalities as a positive feeling. With practice you will find that you now feel confident about the thing you used to be negative towards.

Belief and confidence in what you can do may be so strong that it has the power to change the beliefs of everybody in the world. One man's belief did exactly this. Prior to the 6th May 1954 everyone believed that it was impossible for a man to run a sub four minute mile. Scientists and runners all agreed that it could not be done. Even the use of the word barrier in "the four minute barrier" suggested it could not be done. One man however, did believe. Roger Bannister believed that he could break the four minute mile and this belief made all the difference. On that famous day Roger Bannister, with the assistance of pacemakers Chris Chataway and Chris Brasher, ran a mile in a time of 3 minutes 59.4 seconds. It broke the world record but it also changed the opinion of people around the world. People no longer believed that a sub four minute mile was impossible. This change in belief lead to the following amazing achievements in the years that followed:

46 days later Jim Landry of Australia broke the record again. Landry had been trying like Bannister to beat the record but had not achieved it. Once he saw Bannister beat the time he knew and believed it could be done. That belief and confidence lead to him running the once impossible sub four minute mile.

Since then thousands of people have run times under four minutes. In the next thirty years 16 people broke four minutes. By the end of the 20th century the record had been lowered to the time of

3 minutes 43.13 seconds by Hicham El Guerrouj of Morocco. See what can happen when we believe it can be done and we have the confidence in our own ability to do it.

We can do some or all of the following to help us create that winning feeling of confidence and belief.

1. Remember past successes

Remember success that you have had in the past. However, once you have learned from your failures forget about them. Specifically remember the feelings associated with your past successes.

2. Think about what you want to happen

Focus on what you *want* to happen. We very often focus on what we don't want to happen when we worry. You need to always focus on the result you want. A great example of this happens with golfers all the time. They are standing on the tee before driving and they are thinking about avoiding the bunker. They then take the shot and end up in the bunker they are attempting to avoid. They should be thinking about where they want the ball to finish i.e. what they want to happen and not, what they don't want.

3. Feel Joy and happiness at your successes

When you have successes in your life take the time to enjoy them. No matter how small a success or in what area of your life it occurs you should stop for a moment and experience the feeling fully. Get a real sense of how you feel when you have success. Use as many senses as you can so see what it looks like, sounds like, tastes like, smells like and most importantly what it feels like. When you are enjoying this feeling of confidence and success than create an anchor as we did earlier in the book. Then you can use this anchor to recreate those fantastic feelings.

4. Forget your failures

People often dwell on their past failures and constantly relive them. This as we know is a mistake as we are then thinking about what we don't want. When we have a difficulty or a failing we should take a moment to take on board what we have learned from the situation. Then we need to forget about it. By doing this we can set our minds up to see it as a positive because we have learned something from the experience.

5. Fake it until you make it

There will be times when you are doing things for the first time and you will have no past experience and success to draw upon to create the feelings of confidence and success that you want. In this case you need to draw on your imagination. Imagine yourself in the situation that you will face and see yourself performing exactly the way you want to. Then feel what that is like and hey presto you have created the feelings you desire and those feelings lead to your success.

6. Practice

Practice this as often as possible so that you can create an abundance of confidence and a feeling of success at will. Practice not only instils it in our brains but also in every fibre of our body. You often hear people talk about "feeling it in their gut". This is exactly what we want to create. We want the feeling of confidence flowing through our entire being.

So before moving on to the next chapter please do the following to create that brilliant successful feeling and be full of confidence.

- Pick a successful situation or action from your past. You can pick a different one each time if you are fortunate enough to have many to pick from. If not use your imagination to see yourself performing exactly how you would like to and use that.
- Think about the experience and reactivate the feelings associated with it.
- You will now be feeling confident and the way you want to feel, like a winner. As before use as many of your senses as you can and create a simple anchor.
- Now using your imagination see yourself in your upcoming performances acting and feeling the same way. See yourself using your anchor and feeling the confident feelings flooding through your whole mind and body.
- Practice this regularly
- Complete Step 5 of your My Mentor Me Card with the situations you will use.

The 6th Performance Step – "Getting (over) the Hump"

Overcoming Difficulties

"The greater the obstacle, the more glory in overcoming it."
 Molière

How we deal with problems or issues during our performances can often define how they turn out. In fact performers that deal the best with the bumps or mini crises that inevitably arise are generally speaking the top performers in their fields.

It happens to us all at some stage. A problem comes up, something that we have not foreseen or planned for. It breaks our focus and puts us off track. We begin to focus on what has gone wrong. We are then concentrating our attention on what we don't want and not on our goal. This can lead to a downward spiral that ruins our entire performance.

The good thing for us all is that this happens to everybody no matter what field or area they are performing in. It's normal. It will happen regardless of how well you have prepared. We have seen earlier in the book that we try to foresee issues that will arise when we are visualising. We see ourselves improving our performance in a calm and skilled manner. However there will always be unforeseen events that will occur. It's how we deal with the setbacks that's important and can in fact define the outcome or success of our performance.

It can even be a fantastic opportunity. That single moment where you manage to overcome adversity can become a pivotal time in your career or life. It can be the opportunity to show to everybody how good you really are. You could display skills that not only allow you to overcome that issue but could be the very making of you as a person. There will however always be some issues that we have not anticipated that will require us to deal with them in an efficient manner that allows us to continue to perform to the very best of our ability.

So how do we learn to mentally overcome these problems that arise? We can do some or all of the following to help us deal with those humps and bumps.

1. Visualise

As we have mentioned visualising possible problems enables you to plan solutions as to how you will handle the situation when they occur. So a tennis player might imagine an umpire's call going against them. They might visualise themselves taking a moment using their deep breathing and power statement along with an anchor of bouncing the ball five times. Then they would see themselves focusing on the very next point.

2. Interrupt the pattern

You need to be able to interrupt what is happening in your thought process when a problem occurs. Once you disrupt the unhelpful pattern you can refocus on what you need to do (see 4th Performance Step "Be Here Now". The best way to interrupt the pattern is to do or say something radically different to what you normally would do in the situation to change your focus or physiology. A very simple example is if you are feeling sad, look up, picture Homer Simpson and say the words "Doh". This will interrupt the process of feeling sad and in most cases bring a smile or at least a good feeling to you.

3. Hit the Reset button

It is essential that when we have challenges during our performance that we get back into the correct frame of mind as quickly as possible. In order to do this effectively we need to have a metaphorical "Reset" button. We do this after we have interrupted the destructive pattern. What we want to achieve here is that we have stopped the negative pattern, we have forgotten about it and we have reset our minds and bodies back to our ideal performance state. Again this can be done in any number of ways. It's a question of what works for each individual. One way is to actually imagine hitting a big reset button in your mind that brings about the feelings you want to have as you perform. Another can be a simple action like a golfer removing and putting his glove back on. The magnificent golfer Tiger Woods who most people would agree is one of the most mentally tough sports people around is absolutely excellent at this. He is able to forget about bad shots and get back into his ideal state immediately for the next shot. Some people have suggested that he does a deliberate series of blinks which are possibly part of his hitting his Reset button.

4. Learn from the experience

We often learn the most and progress the most from our mistakes or difficulties. This is a fact of life. It is essential that each time we face a difficulty in our chosen field that we learn from it so that ideally when we face a similar situation in the future we are prepared to deal with it. So it is important that we analyse our performance to see how we could have handled the difficulty better. There is no benefit in doing this while we are still performing. Do it afterwards when we can be more circumspect about it. Make sure not to make mountains out of molehills by over emphasising a particular issue. Do not dwell on it. Most sports or endeavours will beat you up enough so don't beat yourself up also.

So before moving on to the next chapter please do the following to ensure you have your skills honed to deal with issues that arise during your performance.

- Come up with a pattern interrupt for various situations you may face. Ideally come up with something you say and something you do with your body. Make it fun or outrageous as that will work best to really disrupt the pattern of poor thinking before it causes more of a problem.
- Decide on what your "Reset" button is going to be.
- Get a notebook or use your phone to record what you have learned from a situation so that you can apply it the next time.
- Record what your Reset button and pattern interrupt are in Step 6 of your My Mentor Me Card.

The 7th Performance Step- "Trust your bloody brain mate"

The power of your sub conscious

"Good instincts usually tell you what to do long before your head has figured it out."

Michael Burke

A vital element of peak performance is that we let go and trust ourselves to perform to our ability. Specifically we want to bypass the critical part of our mind and allow our sub conscious mind to be in control of our actions. Let's start by talking about what the sub conscious is.

There are two distinct parts to our mind, the conscious and the sub conscious. The conscious mind is the thinking part, the critical factor. It reasons and questions. It has free will and therefore has the ability to reject or accept ideas. It can tell the difference between what is real and what is imagined. It is the part that can question and query why we are doing things in a certain way. It's that nagging voice that we sometimes hear during our performance. It needs to be kept occupied or calmed in order to allow us to get into the zone or flow state. We do that by allowing our sub conscious mind come to the fore.

The subconscious is the emotional part of your mind. It accepts everything that is accepted and passed to it by the conscious mind. It cannot differentiate between what is real and what is imagined. It is the area that stores the vast treasures of our memories, thoughts, actions, teachings and feelings. It is the part of the mind that remembers how we do things and will allow us do things by habit without thinking. It gets us in that flow state or the zone where we do things almost automatically while our conscious mind is occupied.

The best example I always give to people to illustrate the difference between our conscious and sub conscious is that of learning a skill. Take learning to drive. When we first learn to drive we need to think of every single act. Turn the key, put in gear, check the rear view mirror, release the hand break, check the mirror again, foot on the accelerator, ease the clutch and move off. During this period we are thinking consciously of each action and it is somewhat stilted and does not flow easily. I am sure like me you often stalled the car when you were first learning. Then at some stage in the learning process it gets passed over to our subconscious mind which results in us being able to drive without thinking. I am sure we have all experienced a time where we have driven home while our mind has been occupied worrying about something or other. We arrive at our front door without realising how we got there. We drove automatically or rather the automatic part of our mind took care of the driving while our conscious mind was occupied. We negotiated traffic, pedestrians, navigated, obeyed traffic signals and operated the car all without consciously thinking about it. You can rest assured that you will have driven perfectly because you trusted your subconscious mind and allowed yourself to act in that flow state. This is exactly what we want to do when we perform to our very best. How do we go about using and trusting our subconscious mind while occupying our conscious?

1. Set Goals

In order for the subconscious mind to operate it needs goals to be set for it. We need to think about what it is we want to achieve. We need to imagine and create a picture in our heads that we turn over to the subconscious mind. This is where the magic of the subconscious comes into play. It does not question the goal that it has been given by the conscious mind. It cannot do so. It accepts the goal as being what is desired by you and your conscious mind. It is important that you see the goal as already having been achieved. Really see it in your imagination as being real, feel what you would feel having achieved it. As I mentioned the subconscious mind cannot tell the difference between the real or imagined. So it treats the imagined goal as if it were real. It then goes to work using all the power that it has to bring that goal about. It uses all past experiences, knowledge, practice, intuition and skills to bring that imagined goal to life.

Unfortunately we do this all the time very well in a negative way when we worry. We picture something we don't want to come true and we create strong imagined feelings of worry and stress and this comes to pass if we focus on it. So we need to become more expert at using it in more positive ways. We do this by picturing the goal or thing we want as already having been achieved. We feel the feelings associated with it. Then we allow the subconscious to guide us towards our desired goal. In the vernacular "We become what we think about". This leads to those wining feelings that lead us to success.

2. Trust it

Once we have fixed our goal in the subconscious mind it is important that we then trust it to attain that goal for us. We need to allow it to act and to perform what it needs to do in order to bring about what we desire. This means that we need to follow our intuition and trust gut feelings we have as these are the means in which the subconscious guides us. We have to trust our bodies and our muscle memory to carry out our performance perfectly in the way we have done in practice in the past and in our imaginations during visualisation exercises.

3. Occupy your conscious mind.

Obviously we cannot turn off the chattering or the critical element of the conscious mind but what we can do is keep it occupied. This will have a calming effect and allow the sub conscious to enable the mind and body to work in perfect harmony to achieve that flow state. We cannot hold two thoughts in the conscious at once so if we occupy it with a particular thought or task then it cannot be critical of our performance or actions. The best way to achieve this is to come up with something simple or mundane for the conscious mind to do. It can be something related to your performance or it can be something outside of it. While I am sailing in order to occupy my conscious mind I make sure the conscious is in charge of monitoring the compass headings. Ideally it just observes the numbers changing as the wind direction oscillates.

Another technique used by people who are scared of flying is to take sheets of paper with multiplication tables written on the page without the answer filled in. They take something difficult like 19 times tables. Then as they wait on the plane if the worrisome or fearful thoughts start to happen they just start filling in the answers. This occupies the conscious perfectly. Actually the worse you are at maths the better this exercise is as your conscious mind has to work harder.

So before moving on to the next chapter please do the following to ensure you have developed a routine or skill to employ to quieten your conscious and allow your subconscious to perform.

- Come up with goals for your subconscious to focus on. Focus on what you want and not on what you don't want. Create a picture of that goal as if it has already been achieved. Feel what that feels like. Feel the success and confidence that gives you. Do this regularly and you will find that your subconscious will work away at bringing the goal into reality. Do it just before going to bed at night as it is believed that the thoughts we have before we sleep are replayed during the night. So why not make them something good rather than something we worry about.

- Develop a means of occupying your conscious mind and thereby calming it. This can be practiced beforehand using your breathing technique that we mentioned earlier. Also try using hypnosis or meditation, which are very effective and calming the mind. Make sure it is something easy to do in the situation you find yourself, similar to the multiplication tables to quell the thought of worry and fear in a nervous flyer.

- **Record what your means of quietening your conscious are in Step 7 of your My Mentor Me Card.**

PART 2

"If he/she can do it so can I"

In this second part of the book I will give you some examples of how the ideas and techniques of *The Performance Manifesto* are put into practice. I have used some major sporting performances as examples because people will be familiar with them and can research them further should they wish to. In most cases I have used situations where the individuals and teams were really up against it but managed to execute amazing levels of performance. However I do want to stress that the seven steps can be used in your everyday life. You can use it to perform better in work situations like meetings or presentations. Use it for your hobbies, sports, exercise, training, acting, family occasions or any other area of your life that you want to improve in.

Chapter 8 - The Greatest Sporting Comeback of all Time?

It was in the lesser known sport of sailing that witnessed one of the greatest sporting comebacks of all time. This took place in 2013 at the 34th Americas Cup regatta in the waters of San Francisco bay. Spectators around the world were fortunate to witness this event through the magic of new technology. This technology enabled screen viewers to capture the excitement of the racing via superb graphic displays of the racecourse, onboard and head cameras and the telemetry displays from the amazing new catamaran boats. These spectacular boats sailed faster than the speed of the wind. The 90 feet long behemoths appeared to hover on foils no bigger than a surf board. It was even better for those in attendance as the racecourse was mere metres from the San Francisco shorefront allowing the sailors to hear the raucous cheers of their supporters.

The America's Cup is the oldest international sporting trophy in the world dating back to the first race in 1851. It is affectionately known as the "Auld Mug". One yacht, known as the defender, represents the yacht club that currently holds the

America's Cup and the second yacht, known as the challenger, represents the yacht club that is challenging for the cup. In the 2013 Americas cup the match was between challenger Emirates Team New Zealand and Oracle Team USA.

This was a fascinating challenge. At first glance it appeared to be a classic case of David versus Goliath. On paper the might of USA with a seemingly unlimited budget provided by one of the richest men in the world Oracle Chief Larry Ellison seemed to give a huge advantage to Team USA over the tiny nation of New Zealand (Kiwis) with a much smaller budget. The budget allied to the fact that the defender got the right to pick the venue and the type of boat really favoured the home team. However the Kiwis are regarded as the best sailors in the world and make up large parts of every team that has challenged for the America's cup over the last thirty years. In almost every previous America's Cup the fastest boat won. This would prove to be the case once again at the 34th running of the races.

The Kiwis won the right to challenge Oracle Team USA by defeating the other challengers, Artemis from Sweden and Luna Rossa from Italy, in the

Louis Vuitton Cup. They remained unbeaten as they entered the America's Cup Match.

The America's Cup is won by the first boat to win nine races. Against the odds Emirates Team New Zealand lead 8-1, appearing to have a significant advantage. Oracle faced odds of 700 to 1 to make a comeback. However as I mentioned this was possibly the greatest comeback in sporting history. Oracle needed to win eight races in a row against what appeared to be a faster boat. Amazingly they did exactly that and went on to retain the America's cup by a score of 9-8. How did Oracle Team USA bring about this amazing turn around in their performance?

Sailing at this level is highly technical and especially so with the cutting edge technology used in these ultra modern boats. So obviously Oracle were able to make changes to improve the performance of their boat significantly in order to win the cup. However I will be concentrating on how they mentally managed to perform brilliantly. Specifically I will show how they used some of the concepts of the Performance Manifesto to help them.

As with all major sporting events there was a large press conference within an hour of the finish of each race. At these conferences the skipper and one other main crew members faced the world's press. Jimmy Spithill the Australian skipper of Oracle had to attend each time under the most intense pressure imaginable. Each and every time when his team was beaten and on their way to the 8-1 deficit he said "I think we can win". He almost seemed delusional to keep saying that they could overcome the huge odds facing them. He repeated each day while sitting a few feet away from his opposing skipper Dean Barker of Team New Zealand. This was his **Power statement** which he kept repeating over and over again. We can only assume that he was constantly repeating this to himself at all times other than in the glare of the media.

Just to remind you what we discussed earlier in the book about what we are saying to ourselves.

"Our self talk is critical in our belief about our ability to perform. It pervades what we do before, during and after performance. It's what we are saying to ourselves about ourselves, the situation, the competition, our team etc. The type of self talk to a large degree determines the level of our

confidence. Good, positive self talk leads to good, positive levels of confidence and vice versa which leads to improves performance".

This positive self talk by Spithill showed that he believed his team could win, but it also rubbed off on his team mates and was a factor in enabling them to turn around a desperate situation and win the America's cup.

There were two other things that came out that Spithill was doing that I believe helped improve performance. Each night he would look at video footage of the races to see if he could glean any knowledge that could help him. This was an excellent tool to help him ***Visualise on steroids.*** In fact it lead him to believe that they needed to change the way they set the boat for the upwind legs of the races. This was critical to their success as they began sailing at a greater angle to the wind but with enough extra speed to make them faster around the course.

The other thing Spithill was doing was listening to his favourite band Rage Against the Machine on his iPod. While I cannot claim to be a fan of the band titles like "Take the Power Back" and "Immortality" were clearly good for changing the mood and mentality of Spithill. This is a perfect example of changing your physiology to change your thinking or **Shaking your Booty** as we say in The Performance Manifesto.

In my opinion Oracle Team USA also demonstrated brilliantly how to get over a problem and move on or in the vernacular to **Get over the Hump**. Following race 5 Oracle made the call to use their postponement card. This was a rule that each team could call a postponement of a race once during the series. It was intended for teams to use if they had some sort of gear failure and required time to fix it. It was never thought that a team would use it to halt the charge of their opponent. This is the call that Jimmy Spithill and Oracle team CEO Russell Coutts made. At the press conference, the gritty Australian Spithill said: "We feel like we need to regroup, really take a good look at the boat."

This hitting of the metaphorical reset button allowed Oracle to make some changes and to refocus on what they wanted to do. They made modifications to the boat, the way they sailed it upwind and replaced the tactician with Sir Ben Ainslie the four times Olympic gold medal winner.

They spent the day practicing the new sailing mode.

What a transformation! They returned and were now the faster boat and went on to complete this remarkable reversal of fortune. It certainly was the greatest comeback in the history of the America's Cup and maybe in sporting history. They would never have done it if they had not interrupted the existing pattern, hit the reset button and re-focused on what they could control and what they were good at.

Chapter 9 - The Miracle at Medinah

The 39th edition of golf's Ryder Cup held at Medinah near Chicago between the USA and Europe was a close run thing with 14 ½ points to 13 ½ point victory for the Europeans. However the score does not even begin to tell the story of this fantastic competition. The Ryder Cup is one of the rare opportunities for the world's top golfers to play as part of a team. When you add in the team versus individual dynamic to the colour, patriotism and cheering crowds it provides a wonderful cocktail of sporting nirvana. This Ryder Cup provided all this and more.

The American team appeared to hold all the cards. Eleven of the top twelve players in the world were on the US team. A number of the European team were not playing at their best. The USA team enjoyed home course advantage and the support of 40,000 roaring fans. The Ryder Cup however, is the most unpredictable and fascinating of sporting events.

The American team lead 10-4 late on Saturday afternoon having comprehensively outplayed the European team in the four balls and foursomes matches of the first two days. There were two four ball matches to be completed and this is where the tide changed. The talisman for the European team was Englishman Ian Poulter who was partnered with World number 1 Rory McIlroy. Poulter reeled off five successive birdies to win another point for the European team. This along with the point won by the Sergio Garcia and Luke Donald pairing meant that the Europeans went into the singles matches on Sunday 10-6 down and needing to with 8 matches from 12 to retain the Ryder cup.

That evening is where the European minds changed. Poulter returned to the locker room to his team mates singing "There's only one Ian Poulter". This was not your typical losing dressing room. Poulter had earlier described the European challenge as "having a pulse". More importantly he had given the belief to his team mates that they could win. This was borne out by team captain Jose Maria Olazabal's comment "last night when we were having our team meeting I think the boys understood that believing was the most important thing.

Sunday and the singles matches saw Olazabal take the brave decision to front load his team by putting out his top players first. His intention was to take early points and turn the all important momentum the way of the European team. He achieved this in spectacular fashion with Europe taking the first five points. This gave the requisite boost to the entire team and allowed German Martin Kaymer to take the plaudits as the player who sunk the winning put that meant Europe retained the cup. This was a huge turnaround in fortune. How did it happen?

As with the America's Cup comeback I will take you through some of the ways in which Captain Olazabal and his team used the ideas we have discussed in The Performance Manifesto to ensure they took the Ryder cup back to Europe.

A huge factor in the European win was that the players were emotionally involved in the fight to win. This was achieved and referenced often by the players and Olazabal. Captain Olazabal and the wider world of golf had lost the mercurial talents of Seve Ballesteros shortly before the Ryder Cup. Ballesteros was a Ryder cup winning player, former captain and playing partner to Olazabal in previous editions of the cup. He was also a great friend of Olazabal's and was a huge influence on all the European players. In an emotional speech by Olazabal the night before the singles matches

Olazabal urged his charges to "do it for Seve". This became the focus of their self talk, their **Power Statement**. Ballesteros name was evoked to inspire the Europeans. In addition it was evident in the European team's visualization of Seve as his silhouette was on the sleeves of the European shirts and golf bags. In addition the Europeans wore navy and white, the colours most readily associated with Seve. This was a powerful tool to help the European team visualise their success. It was evidenced by Sergio Garcia a fellow Spaniard when he said "I have no doubt in my mind that he (Ballesteros) was with me today all day because there was no way I would have won my match today if he wasn't there". When you are visualizing recently deceased heroes in this manner you are definitely *visualising* at a powerful level or *On steroids* as we say. Graeme McDowell of Northern Ireland also pointed out "Jose wanted to win it for Seve and we wanted to win it for Jose and Seve. A light aircraft was also seen flying overhead with a banner "Do it for Seve".

Olazabal showed his confidence on Saturday evening by declaring "I still believe". This along with an emotional speech at the team meeting on

Saturday evening that saw a number of the team in tears instilled a huge level of confidence in every member of the team. This was further enhanced by looking at video of past successes at the Ryder cup.

The European team successfully **got over the hump** in a very positive manner. Poulter and Mc Ilroy's success and the chants that greeted them on their return to the locker room served to break the negative pattern that they had gotten into. This break was also strengthened by the fact that the players had the night to sleep on it. The new pattern of joy, confidence and focus was installed in the players' minds during the buoyant scenes in the locker room and at the team dinner. This was then magnified by the early turning blue of the scoreboard as Europe took the all important wins in the early singles matches. The German Martin Kaymer epitomized this when he spoke of his discussion with Captain Olazabal during his match. Olazabal told Kaymer on the 16th hole that he would need the point win from his match to win the Ryder cup. Kaymer said that "I loved that feeling, loved it". He duly delivered the winning put under massive pressure on the final hole. A truly amazing performance by all concerned.

Chapter 10 - The Revival under the Roof

The next example of brilliant performance is the Heineken Rugby Cup final between Irish team Leinster and English team Northampton Saints on 21st May 2011. The Heineken Cup is the European championship of club Rugby. That year's final was played under the enclosed roof of the magnificent Millennium stadium in Cardiff, Wales in front of 72,000 loyal and noisy fans.

This was to prove another remarkable game involving a truly superb comeback. Northampton dominated the first half to lead 22-6 at half time following tries from Phil Dowsen, Ben Foden and Dylan Hartley. Two of the three tries were converted by Stephen Myler to add to his one successful penalty kick. Leinster's only reply was two penalties from outhalf Jonathan Sexton which left the Irish side in a desperate situation.

Leinster came out for the second half like men possessed. They played amazing Rugby to completely reverse roles and dominate Northampton. In one of the most remarkable turnarounds, Leinster scored 27 points in the second half, and held Northampton scoreless, to win the match 33–22. Any notion that Leinster were down and out of this magnificent match were dispelled in a scintillating 13 minute period following the start of the second half. That was the time it took for Sexton to score 14 points, converting both of his own tries, as Leinster fought their way back. Then Sexton also kicked a penalty in the 57th minute to give Leinster a one point lead. Another penalty from Sexton and a try from Nathan Hines gave Leinster the victory. Northampton had no answer to the dominant men in blue.

As with the previous examples I will take you through some of the things which Leinster did to bring about this extraordinary transformation in performance.

The key thing that Leinster did was maintain their belief at half time in themselves and that they could still win the game. This was illustrated by a number of the leaders in the team. After the match, Leinster and Ireland legendry centre Brian O'Driscoll revealed that it was the flyhalf (Sexton) that sparked the team's unbelievable comeback. "Besides what Jonny produced in the second half, some of his words at half-time really struck a chord. He was a man possessed. He said this game would be remembered if we came back. You could see he had the bit between his teeth and he was ready for it." Sexton told his teammates that stranger things have happened in sport and that they only needed to think back to Liverpool's 3-0 down recovery in the 2005 Champions League Final to see that the impossible is indeed, possible. He said that if they did comeback it would be remembered forever.

"We were shell-shocked and we needed half-time. We regrouped," Sexton explained. "I'm a bit of a nerd when it comes to sport and I said we see in sport that teams can come back, like Liverpool a few years ago. Stuff like that happens. We had to believe it."

This illustrated the belief that Sexton had which rubbed off on his team mates following his rousing speech. This was further reinforced by the storming start to the second half made by Leinster and in particular Sexton. Using the two tools of *visualisation* and *belief* the Leinster players were filled with confidence.

Enda Mc Nulty the Leinster sports psychologist highlighted a couple of things that he felt were instrumental in his team's performance.

He felt that the team's confidence and belief came from their mental toughness which had been forged from 2008 onwards. They were able to recall the tough situations they had been in before and be confident that they could perform. This allied to their superb fitness and conditioning proved a lethal cocktail.

He believed that the body language of his players was always positive. He used the example of Leinster fullback Isa Nacewa's reaction to the Foden try. He simply just moved to his position for the next play seemingly unperturbed. *"Shaking his booty"* as we would say but in a more understated Kiwi fashion.

He also praised the focus of his team as they remained in the *here and now* by concentrating on what they could control. That was executing their basic skills under the massive pressure of a major final. Greg Feek the forwards coach noted an issue in the scrum which was addressed and resulted in an improved scrum which provided Leinster with the platform to get the scores they needed.

Mc Nulty also highlighted the magnificent support and noise of the supporters which was enhanced by the Millennium stadium's roof remaining closed. All these factors contributed to Leinster *getting over the hump* of their first half performance.

All in all an amazing performance. If you get the chance it is well worth watching.

Chapter 11 - Putting it all together

In order to illustrate the seven steps of The Performance Manifesto in action I am going to use the example of giving a speech or a presentation. This is something that most people have to do at some stage in their lives. It is also something a large number of people struggle with. The way that I suggest below is not set in stone. It is imperative that you feel comfortable with it so feel free to use all the suggestions below or modify it to your own personal style. I have also included an example of a My Mentor Me card to help you. Further examples used by some of my clients are available on my website www.theperformancemanifesto.com .

Power Statement

So the first thing to consider is what sort of speech you will be giving. Is it a professional presentation, a teaching class, a speech at a wedding or a eulogy? Obviously these examples would be completely different in terms of tone. You also need to consider the age and sex of the audience. The next thing to consider is the topic. Is it a heavy going high on detail dry topic or more light hearted and funny. You need to consider how well the audience knows the topic in terms of what level of detail you go in to. Once you have considered these things you will have a much better idea of the essence of what your speech is all about and how you want to feel during it.

So for the professional presentation you might decide that you want to feel calm, professional and knowledgeable. Whereas, for a eulogy you might want to be sincere, sad but in control. So these are the words that you would use as your ***Power statement***. So you write these down in you're My Mentor Me card.

Also choose an anchor that you can use during the speech to recall these feelings. So for this example we will use the anchor of rubbing our thumb and index finger together. So when we practice saying our Power statement we also rub the fingers together when we are in the state that we desire so that we can do the same during our speech to immediately bring those feelings forth.

Visualisation

We need to develop a visualization exercise that sees us being successful. So we will use all the steps of *Visualising on Steroids* to create an effective and useful tool for us.

First you need to see yourself as being successful and having the desired state or feelings that you have decided on in your Power statement. Then you need to create a mental movie of this happening. You need to see the movie from your own point of view or through you own eyes as opposed to looking down from above. You also need to see the situation in as much detail as you can and to utilize as many senses as you can. So in your mental movie see the room, see the audience reaction, and see your presentation notes or slides. Feel the microphone in your hand, feel the temperature in the room. Hear the audience laughing or reacting in the manner you want or expect. If it is possible imagine the smell. For example you might imagine the smell of incense or flowers in a church.

Then you need to run through the scenario right the way through to the end. You may find that something is not quite right so just rerun it in your mind until it is right and exactly as you wish it to be.

Use past experiences or successful speeches you have given in the past as part of your visualisation. Pick the best ones and include them.

Then project yourself into the future and see yourself performing exactly as you want to. See people applauding, smiling, shaking your hand and saying what a good job you did. While you are doing this exercise you will be feeling the feelings you want to have during the speech so don't forget to repeat your Power statement and rub your fingers together to anchor those feeling.

Now put a short description of the scenarios you will use during your visualization in you're my Mentor Me card which will help you to practice.

Shake your Booty (Body Movement & Breathing)

We want to use our bodies to help us get into our desired state or to shake us out of an unwanted state of mind. So the state of mind we want for our speech could be to be calm and confident. So I would use deep breathing exercise to achieve this calm feeling. I would use it during my practice, my visualization, prior to and during performance. I would also use this alongside my power statement and anchor that I have previously decided upon.

In addition to my breathing I would also come up with another anchor that I could use to energise myself. This would be particularly useful if your presentation or speech was going to go on for some time and your energy or excitement levels may wane. This could be something like rubbing your hands together vigorously or clapping your hands together. We would set this up by simply imagining ourselves feeling energised and then clapping our hands. In addition clap our hands together at times when we are feeling energised. This sets up the powerful link or anchor that when we clap our hands we are energised. So that now when we are speaking and our energy is diminishing we can just clap our hands and that energised feeling will come flooding back to us when we need it.

So complete number three, Shake your Booty on you're my Mentor Me card with the actions you have decided upon

Be Here Now (Focus)

Once again in order to keep focussed on the task and being here and now we will use the techniques to keep us feeling relaxed and calm. So that's our breathing, power statement, anchors and body movements.

We need to concentrate on the process not the outcome. We need to focus on what we can control not on the outcome. So in the case of our speech we can concentrate on things like the tone of our voice, the cadence, volume and pace of our talking. Do not pay attention to the outcome or the impact that our speech is having.

Also it is important that we don't evaluate or judge our speech as we are making it. We can do this more effectively after we have finished as we will be able to gauge the feedback and be more objective in our assessment.

So now complete point four, Be Here Now in you're My Mentor Me card with what you are going to focus on.

Day Dreaming for adults (Confidence and & Belief)

As we deliver our speech or presentation we want to feel confident and believe that we are doing a good job. That confidence comes from within us. As a result we can create that feeling of confidence. We do this in two ways using our amazing minds and imaginations.

The first is that we recall past successes if we have previous experiences to draw upon. We simply recall those events in as much detail and get a real sense of how that success feels. Once again this works best when we use all our senses and we anchor that feeling of confidence in both our minds and bodies. Once we can feel successful confident beliefs that we can do it we can easily recreate them.

The second is to use our imagination to see ourselves giving that speech and doing it confidently and in exactly the way we want to do it. We should do this following the recalling of past successes so that we can carry that confident feeling with us. It is imperative that we concentrate on what we want to happen and not worry about what might go wrong.

Also if you do not have experience to draw upon just use your mind to imagine how it will feel. As I said the feeling comes from within us so we can create it. It is not dependent on external factors.

As you practice delivering your speech, remember to practice these confidence and belief exercises also. The double whammy of practice and the feeling of confidence will make you feel unstoppable.

Now go and complete point 5, Day Dreaming for Adults on your My Mentor Me card with the feelings you want and the past experiences you are going to use for this exercise.

Getting over the Hump (Overcoming difficulties)

No matter how well we have prepared in terms of our practice and our mental preparation we will inevitably have a difficulty or problem that we have to overcome during our performance. We must first attempt to reduce these to a minimum but also we need to plan and prepare for how we will deal with them when they do inevitably arise. Also overcoming these difficulties allows us to really develop and become better at whatever it is we are doing.

In the case of our speech we have included trying to foresee problems during our visualization practice. We predict a possible difficulty and also see ourselves dealing with the problem in an effective manner. We also need to prepare for how we will deal with unforeseen issues.

We need to do two things. The first is we need to put in place our technique for interrupting our thought pattern when things go wrong. So for example if the projector were to break down our initial thoughts might be to think this is a disaster. We need to interrupt this pattern of thought as quickly as possible. We have to come up with something simple that we can do in the moment that stops this thought pattern in its tracks. So a simple gesture like a clapping of the hands or a light pinch is ideal. It just needs to be something that takes our attention away from the bad thought process.

Second, we then have to restart our desired state of mind and feelings. We do this by "hitting the restart button". This can be simply imagining hitting a big restart button in your head and imagining this kicking off your desired feelings. In the case of the speech it could be something physical like picking up your cue cards (which you prepared in case the projector broke down) and imagine calm confidence flooding back through you.

Lastly we need to learn from the difficulty that arose. It will be the confidence that is built in you as a result of overcoming these difficulties that will make you even better the next time.

So once again please complete point 6, Getting Over the Hump in you're my Mentor Me Card. Put in your chosen pattern interrupt and your preferred reset button.

"Trust your bloody Mind Mate"

We have prepared and practiced our speech. We have done all the previous six steps of The Performance Manifesto. We have completed our My Mentor Me card and carry it with us to practice regularly when we have a few spare minutes. Now we need to hand it over to our subconscious mind and trust it to execute our task perfectly.

We need to first set our goal. In the case of a professional speech it could be to impart certain key knowledge in a clear and concise manner. Whereas a wedding speech could be to tell the guests about the bride, groom, son or daughter while conveying how much you love them and how happy you are for them on their big day.

Once the conscious mind has decided upon the goal the subconscious mind accepts it and will act in a way to achieve it. We do this by imagining that it has already been achieved and experiencing how that feels. In this simple manner we become what we think about.

Then you need to trust yourself to execute it perfectly. This means listening and being aware of hints that you get via your intuition or gut feeling and acting upon them.

Lastly we need to come up with something to occupy our conscious mind so we can stop its critical factor. This could be something like focusing on your grip of the microphone if you are using one and making sure your grip is relaxed. You could have it focus on your presentation slides. It just needs to be a simple action or thing that takes the focus of your conscious mind away from questioning or being critical so you can allow yourself to perform brilliantly.

Chapter 12 - Just Do it Regularly

"Excellence is an art won by training and habituation. We do not act rightly because we have virtue or excellence, but we rather have those because we have acted rightly. We are what we repeatedly do. Excellence, then, is not an act, but a habit".

Aristotle

These wise words, written by the philosopher and scientist Aristotle around 350BC, are as relevant today as they were then. They encapsulate exactly what I want to teach you about practice. Practice is not something you do once in a while. It is something that needs to be done every day in order to achieve brilliant performance. It is best to keep your practice of the 7 Steps of The Performance Manifesto to about ten minutes a day and to do it every day. The cumulative effect of this daily exercise will build great momentum and improve your confidence levels no end.

I would highly recommend reading Jeff Olson's fantastic book "The Slight Edge". His book is about having a philosophy that doing simple daily tasks will inevitably lead to massive success. In his words "little productive actions repeated consistently over time add up to the difference between success and failure". It is this idea that we will apply to the practice of the Seven Steps.

I suggest that your practice sessions are kept to less than ten minutes and that it is essential that you do them daily. I would hope that as a result of carrying your My Mentor Me card with you, it will enable you to practice anytime you have a spare few moments. Here is a brief outline of what a practice session might look like:

- Take out your My Mentor Me Card
- Read through the steps and hear your Power statement out loud a few times.
- Then close your eyes and take ten deep breaths to help you to relax.
- Repeat your Power statement as you continue to relax.
- Visualize your upcoming performance happening exactly as you want it to happen. Take your cue from the feelings you wanted to feel that are written on your MMM card.
- Anchor this feeling with the anchor you have on your card.

- See you yourself carrying out your focus technique that you have decided upon and written on your card.
- Run through some past successes in your mind. If you have no previous experience, don't worry. Just imagine a number of different scenarios in which you are successful.
- Now imagine your future success.
- See yourself coming up against a problem and imagine dealing with it brilliantly.
- See yourself using whatever it is that you have set as your "reset" button.
- Then see yourself continuing on and performing brilliantly.

Remember to continuously adjust and amend your practice until it is perfect. Perfect practice will lead to a brilliant performance. Then after you have completed your performance and it has gone well don't forget to incorporate that experience in your practice for the next time. Each success will build on the next one.

Olson talks about book smarts and street smarts in the Slight Edge. What he is getting at is that our knowledge from book learning is enhanced by actually going out and doing it. Each performance is influenced by the book learning and then the next learning and practice after the performance is improved. It is a continuous circle of book learning, doing, learning again following the doing.

To paraphrase a well know slogan "Just do it (regularly).

Appendix 1 - Short User Guide

Short User Guide to The Performance Manifesto and My Mentor Me Card

This is a synopsis of the book which allows readers to start using The Seven Steps right away or for somebody who just wants a quick refresher of the steps in the process.

Step 1 The Power Statement

Devise a short statement or series of relevant words to your performance that describe your desired state. The aim is to create positive self talk. So use the Power statement regularly during your training, practice, visualisation and performance. Create a physical action or anchor that helps recall the positive talk and feelings. Write it down on your My Mentor Me (MMM) card.

Step 2 Visualisation on Steroids

Visualise your performance from your point of view. Use previous positive experiences where you experienced the feelings the way you want. Use as many of your five senses as possible. Visualise yourself performing as you want to in the upcoming event or task. Write it down on your My Mentor Me (MMM) card.

Step 3 Shake your Booty

Change your thinking by changing your physiology. Change what you are doing with your body by moving, taking a number of deep breaths, exercising and eating correctly. These simple steps will improve your performance. Write it down on your My Mentor Me (MMM) card.

Step 4 Be Here Now

In order to keep focus on the present ensure that your keep calm. Focus on some part of the process rather than thinking about the outcomes. Focus on what you can control. Devise a point of focus that you can concentrate your conscious mind on to keep it occupied. Develop a ritual to get you focussed which includes your Power statement, anchor and your breathing. Write it down on your My Mentor Me (MMM) card.

Step 5 Day Dreaming for Adults – Confidence and belief

Confidence is the emotion we as an individual want to feel during our performance. In order to feel confident, recall past successes and in particular the feelings of it. Then anchor that feeling. Then think about what you want to happen. Remember and enjoy your successes. Learn from your failures and then forget them. If you have no positive examples to call on just imagine what it would feel like to feel confident. Write it down on your My Mentor Me (MMM) card.

Step 6 Getting (over) the Hump

How you deal with unforeseen issues that will inevitably arise can define your performance. Therefore visualise any possible problems and see yourself dealing with them. Devise a simple means of interrupting the pattern of thought during a problem. Then come up with an imaginary reset button. Finally learn from these situations so you can deal with them if they come up again. Write it down on your My Mentor Me (MMM) card.

Step 7 Trust your Bloody Mind Mate

It is imperative that you set goals so that your sub conscious mind can work towards them. You need to learn to trust your sub conscious mind and to let go to perform at your very best. Come up with some means of occupying your critical conscious mind. Write it down on your My Mentor Me (MMM) card.

Appendix 2 - My Mentor Me Card (MMM) Example

The following is an example of a MMM card that could be used for a presentation that you need to give. Further examples of the MMM card are available at www.theperformancemanifesto.com.

My Mentor Me Card©

1. **Power Statement**

   Calm, clear & professional.

2. **Visualisation on Steroids**
   Previous successful presentations
   Anchor – rub thumb and fore finger together.

3. **Shake your booty**
   Breathing & standing upright

4. **Be Here Now**
   Focus on the feel of cards in hands or microphone.

5. **Day Dreaming for adults (Confidence & Belief)**
   Use past success in presentations or imagined success.
   Project in your mind to the upcoming presentation.

6. **Get over the Hump**
   Decide on how you are going to interrupt negative pattern.
   Hit imaginary "reset button" in head and say "we go again"

7. **Trust your bloody mind mate**

   Set goal of giving an informative and professional presentation. Trust yourself to execute perfectly.

Appendix 3 - Hypnotic Relaxation Session

I mentioned that I use hypnosis to improve my relaxation and visualisation sessions. Below I provide a simple hypnotic relaxation session. You can also download a copy of my Relaxation session "The Essence of Relaxation" at www.theperformancemanifesto.com Alternatively you can record yourself speaking the script below. Just find a comfortable chair or bed and ensure you won't be disturbed for 20 minutes or so. Make sure that you are not driving or operating machinery as this is a closed eyes exercise. Just enjoy it. It's really relaxing.

You have now volunteered to enter a very pleasant state known as hypnosis, expect to be hypnotised and you will be hypnotised.

Now I want you to pick a spot on the wall and look at it. As you are looking at the spot on the wall you can look forward to a number of changes occurring, some of which you will be aware of, others will be happening at a deeper level.

As you follow my simple instructions, no power in the universe can keep you from entering into a very deep and pleasant state of hypnosis. You have volunteered to be hypnotised, expect to be hypnotised and you will be hypnotised.

Take a deep breath and fill your lungs. Now exhale. That's fine. Now a second and deeper breath... exhale... relax. Now a third deep breath....exhale and relax.

And now I am going to count down from five to one. As I do your eylids grow heavy, droopy, drowsy and sleepy. By the time I reach the count of one, they close right down and you go into a hypnotic slumber deeper than you have ever previously experienced. Alright......

5   Eyelids heavy, droopy, drowsy and sleepy.

4   Those heavy eyelids feel ready to close.

3   The next time you blink, that's hypnosis coming on you now.

2   They begin closing, closing, closing, close them, close them.

1 They're closing, closing, closing...... sleep now!

Just relax and go deeply into hypnosis, deeper than you have ever previously experienced.

Your eyes are so tightly closed that the more you try you open them, the tighter they are locking closed. The way you lock them tighter is by relaxing all the tiny little muscles around your eyes. The more relaxed those tiny little muscles are the more tightly shut your eyes remain.

Before you continue to relax and enter onto a deep state of light trance or a light state of deep trance, you may notice that there is a gentle flickering in your eyelids. And this soothing sensation makes you aware that you are entering some delightful space in your mind where time loses its usual meaning, which allows you to perceive so many things in different ways.

Be able now to explore within yourself your thoughts, feelings and many different things that you come to know about yourself with the feelings associated with being comfortable with yourself and the kind of internal absorption that you know you are capable of. Why not allow yourself the luxury of being able to drift along, listening and not listening, a little at a time and make your conscious mind expect the experience of comfort and your unconscious can expect something even deeper, so it won't really matter whether you consciously allow yourself the experience of a very deep, light state of trance, or unconsciously allow yourself a lighter state of deep trance.

As you go deeper now, just listening to the sound of my voice..... you are aware of comfortable heavy feelings of legs, of arms, of the entire body that seems to float in time and space, of hypnotic sensations that allow you that you have move from one state of awareness into another state in a calm and confident way. And I wonder now if you allow those feelings to continue..... those comfortable, relaxed sensations of mind and body....as you drift and dream....and my voice drifts with you.

I want you now to imagine a ruler standing upright in front of you. We are going to use the ruler to measure the depth of your hypnosis. Look at your ruler now to see how close to zero you are. Take a deep breath and say to yourself double my relaxation. Say it again double my relaxation and say it until you reach your basement of relaxation. This will be somewhere close to zero or may even be below zero.

Now imagine opening a door into your safe place. It can be a real place or an imaginary place or a combination of both. Now relax even deeper in your safe place. Ten times deeper ten times deeper. That's right.

Now place your thumb and forefinger together and think the words "I am calm, relaxed, comfortable, in control and confident. From now on when you place your thumb and forefinger together like this you will immediately go down to your basement of relaxation and into your safe place.

Feel your entire body relax now. Enjoy that relaxed feeling flowing from the tips of your toes to the top of your head. Relax deeper and deeper with each wonderful breath.

Relaxation & Confidence Script

Imagine you are walking toward the ocean.... walking through a beautiful, tropical forest.... you can hear the waves up ahead.... you can smell the ocean spray.... the air is moist and warm.... feel a pleasant, cool breeze blowing through the trees....you walk along a path....coming closer to the sea....as you come to the edge of the trees, you see the brilliant blue turquoise aqua colour of the ocean ahead....you walk out of the forest and onto a long stretch of white sand.... the sand is very soft powder.... imagine taking off your shoes, and walking through the soft, white sand toward the water....the beach is wide and long....hear the waves crashing to the shore....smell the clean salt water and beach....you gaze again toward the water.... it is a bright blue-green....see the waves washing up onto the sand..... and receding back toward the ocean.... washing up.... and flowing back down..... enjoy the ever-repeating rhythm of the waves...imagine yourself walking toward the water.... over the fine, warm sand.... you are feeling hot....as you approach the water, you can feel the mist from the ocean on your skin. You walk closer to the waves, and feel the sand becoming wet and firm....a wave washes over the sand toward you.... and touches your toes before receding...as you step forward, more waves wash over your feet... feel the cool water provide relief from the heat....walk further into the clear, clean water.... you can see the white sand under the water.... the water is a pleasant, relaxing temperature.... providing relief from the hot sun... cool but not cold....you walk further into the water if you wish.... swim if you want to.... enjoy the ocean for a few minutes..... allow yourself to deepen your relaxation.... more and more relaxed... enjoy the ocean....now you are feeling calm and refreshed...you walk back out of the water and onto the beach...stroll along the beach at the water's edge.... free of worries... no stress... calm..... enjoying this moment of peace....up ahead is a comfortable towel, just for you...lie down on the towel on the sand.... relax on the towel....

enjoying the sun.... the breeze.... the waves.....the warmth of the sand

You feel peaceful and relaxed.... allow all your stresses to melt away....

As you are relaxing there you fully accept and believe in yourself just the way you are, for you are a unique and special person, and people love and accept you just the way you are.....you are a valuable and important person and you enjoy the respect and friendship that others give you....the more you love yourself the more you are able to love others....you deal with challenges in a positive way....your mind is full of positive thoughts and feelings such as.... you can do it....you are confident, capable, talented, self assured, valuable, important, skilled and successful.....you feel comfortable and confident within yourself, and feel good about the world around you....you feel more self confident whatever you are doing....everyday you are more relaxed, steadier and more confident mentally and physically....you have the knowledge and ability to handle every challenge that comes along in your life....your confidence in yourself and your abilities grow everyday....you are confident in all social situations....you see yourself in your imagination achieving each goal you set, for you are a confident, goal-oriented winner....you now realise that life is good and exciting for you, because you allow your subconscious mind to express your growing confidence....you are a naturally good and confident person, therefore people like you and respect you for who and what you are....you know that there is no such thing as mistakes in life only learning experiences....each and every day you are getting better in every way.... as you look to the future you see positive things occurring in your life, you are calm, relaxed and in control in every situation.

The next time you listen to this recording and close your eyes, you will relax ten times more deeply than you previously experienced....

You will enjoy playing your hypnotic recording on a daily basis and you will find that those good positive suggestions will grow stronger each day that goes by.

Place your thumb and forefinger together and you will instantly be able to drop down to your basement of relaxation

Now when I count from one to five, let your eyelids open. You are calm relaxed, refreshed, rested and feeling wonderfully good.

One, slowly calmly and gently returning to full awareness once again.

Two, each muscle and nerve in your body is loose and limp and relaxed. You feel wonderfully good

Three, from head to toe you are feeling perfect in every way

On number four, your eyes begin to feel sparkling clear just as though they were bathed in cold spring water.

On the next number, let your eyelids open. You are calm, rested, refreshed, relaxed and you feel wonderful.

Number five, eyelids open now, take a deep breath, fill up your lungs, stretch and smile.

www.ingramcontent.com/pod-product-compliance
Lightning Source LLC
Chambersburg PA
CBHW071902020426
42331CB00010B/2637